POLICE SEARCHING PROCEDURES

POLICE
SEARCHING
PROCEDURES

By

J. McCAUSLIN MOYNAHAN, JR., B.S.

Nidan (2nd Degree Black Belt) Okazaki Ju Jitsu

Shodan (1st Degree Black Belt) Shudokan Karate

Ikkyu (1st Degree Brown Belt) Kodokan Judo

Honorary Black Belt, Danish Sports Judo Federation

CHARLES C THOMAS · PUBLISHER
Springfield · Illinois · U.S.A.

Published and Distributed Throughout the World by
CHARLES C THOMAS · PUBLISHER
BANNERSTONE HOUSE
301-327 East Lawrence Avenue, Springfield, Illinois, U.S.A.

© *1963, by* CHARLES C THOMAS · PUBLISHER
Library of Congress Catalog Card Number: 63-13429

*With THOMAS BOOKS careful attention is given to all details of
manufacturing and design. It is the Publisher's desire to present books
that are satisfactory as to their physical qualities and artistic possibilities
and appropriate for their particular use. THOMAS BOOKS will be true
to those laws of quality that assure a good name and good will.*

Printed in the United States of America
H-2

FOREWORD

THIS TEXT IS WRITTEN so that police officers will know and not guess the proper method with which to search a subject.

There are many haphazard methods of searching which cause officers trouble. One officer may "search" a subject and then another may get shot by the same subject while on the way to the police station.

Whether searching for weapons, narcotics or anything else this text will be extremely helpful. Study carefully each method of searching and then apply it to the particular situation.

Searching is a very important duty which must be executed properly. In this area carelessness can be very dangerous.

J. M. M., Jr.

ACKNOWLEDGMENTS

THE AUTHOR'S THANKS goes to all those who have helped in the preparation of this text.

Special thanks goes to those who posed for this text, Larry A. Skeen, David B. Menig, James R. Giovannini and Ernest E. Muir.

My sincere thanks to Steve Nelson for his usual good job in the photographic work for this text.

Finally, much thanks goes to Web Ruble for his editing.

J. M. M., Jr.

CONTENTS

POLICE SEARCHING PROCEDURES

Chapter 1

GENERAL POINTS ON SEARCHING

THE MOST IMPORTANT thing the author has to say is that *any* apprehension is potentially dangerous. It is very difficult for us to know what is going on in a subject's mind at the time of his arrest. All officers must take care in their apprehension of a subject. Even the meekest and mildest man may be extremely resentful and antagonistic when arrested.

If possible get assistance before searching a subject. Two officers insure much more safety than one. It also is advisable not to get too many officers where only one or two subjects are being searched. The old saying, "Too many cooks spoil the broth," is certainly true in searching.

The searching of a subject is aimed at giving the officer the advantage. Don't take chances; if you believe there is any possibility that the subject has a weapon, then search him. It is much better to be overly cautious than to be unsure.

After apprehending a subject, a fast search for readily accessible weapons may be made. Later a frisk search should be utilized. The fast search can be made where there are other people around. Frisk and wall searches should be made in a less public place.

There is a possibility that the subject being searched may have friends looking on. These individuals may be a source of trouble if they become sympathizers. Therefore any search, even a frisk search, should be conducted out of the public view if possible.

Many requests a prisoner may make are often stalls. This is an area where the officer may be extremely susceptible unless he is being very watchful. The officer should attend to the job of searching as soon as possible without wasting any time. He should always give the impression that he knows exactly what to do and that he has any given situation in control.

In arresting and apprehending a prisoner there are certain things which should be examined closely since they will cause the most trouble for the officer.

The first of these important factors is carelessness. The officer can never be too cautious in arresting and/or searching a subject. You never know what is going on in a subject's mind at the time of arrest or search. He may take the situation rather lightly or he may suddenly go psychotic and blow apart.

Don't be careless about searching a subject. Do a thorough job of searching. You may later turn your subject over to another officer. When he asks if your subject is searched you must be able to reply "yes" with confidence.

Over-confidence when searching a prisoner should be avoided. When searching you must remember that the subject is always potentially dangerous. The subject may have no weapons other than his hands but these may be extremely dangerous. Respect your opponent's potential strength.

When searching it is very important to have your attention focused upon your subject. If your attention is attracted to something else, it may give your subject the split second he needs to over power you and possibly escape.

Training may play an important role in your technique. You can never be trained too much. It is necessary that an officer learn the searching techniques properly.

It is important to know how and where to search. Since this book lays down searching techniques in step by step progression, it is very important that this progression is practiced in the same step by step order.

The officer is generally interested in searching for weapons and possibly narcotics. Remember, in most searching techniques it is better to crush the clothing with the hand rather than to pat it. If you pat the clothing you are less likely to find objects.

A more detailed search can be made at the police station with the strip search. This is where the subject sheds all of his clothes and he and the clothes are completely searched. See Chapter Five for the strip search.

In transporting a subject who has been searched it is advisable to cuff him and then run his belt through the cuffs as a safety precaution. This will limit the subject in many ways (Fig. 1).

After all searches where the subject is suspected of a major crime, cuffs should be applied. The meekest lamb may suddenly turn into a tiger while being transported to the police station.

If you are by yourself and it is possible to get aid from another officer before a search, do so. This will place more safety on your side.

This book has been written with the idea that two officers will conduct the search. Therefore all of the illustrations will be demonstrated with two officers present. This does not mean that two officers must be present, for one can easily search a subject.

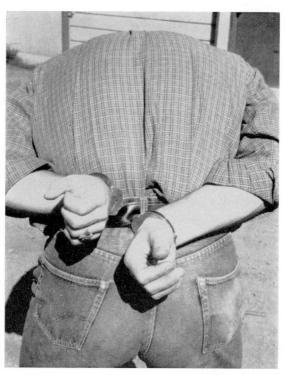

Fig. 1

Chapter 2

THE FRISK SEARCH

THE FRISK SEARCH is a rapid search for obvious weapons. It is also a search which is utilized where there is no wall or car available for searching procedures. (You may have the subject lean against a car while being searched, in place of a wall. Consult the chapter on wall searching.)

In the frisk search, as in other searches, it is very important to crush the clothing with the hand rather than to pat the clothing.

The subject should be told to look straight ahead and say nothing.

Your partner should stand away from the subject and be alert all of the time during the search. It probably is better that your partner should stay in front of the subject being searched.

Remember to search from the rear of the subject. This is psychologically advantageous as he cannot be sure of your location.

The step by step illustrations of the frisk search follow:

A criminal act is attempted or committed (Fig. 2). Two policemen approach the location of the criminal (Fig. 3). One gun is drawn on the subject and preparations are made for a search (Fig. 4).

The subject is instructed to open his hands and hold them high in the air and spread his feet well apart (Fig. 5). Before the subject is searched one officer gets into position to cover him (Figs. 6 and 7). The pistol may be drawn, depending on the officer's judgment.

You begin your search from behind the subject starting with the hat (Fig. 8). Turn hat inside out and search lining (Fig. 9).

Check the subject's neck and collar (Fig. 10). A check should be made under the subject's arm (Fig. 11). Next a check should be made of the upper back (Fig. 12). The lower back should also be checked (Fig. 13).

A check should be made of the upper part of the man's chest and the lower region around the stomach (Figs. 14, 15 and 16). The belt, a favorite concealment spot, also should be checked (Fig. 17). The inside thigh and crotch area also should be searched (Fig. 18). The legs should be checked for possible weapons (Figs. 19, 20 and 21). The last items to be checked are the shoes and cuffs of the subject (Figs. 22, 23 and 24).

The application of hand cuffs should end the frisk search. At this same time the sleeves of the subject can be searched. When applying cuffs, do so gently. Hold on to the other cuff so it is not used as a weapon against you (Figs. 25, 26 and 27).

If necessary, you may grab the cuffs, place your hand on the subject's back and utilize this as a come along (Fig. 28). If pressure is needed you may lift up on the cuffs. When this is applied most subjects become very uncomfortable.

Fig. 2

Fig. 3

Fig. 4

Fig. 5

Fig. 6

Fig. 7

Fig. 8

Fig. 9

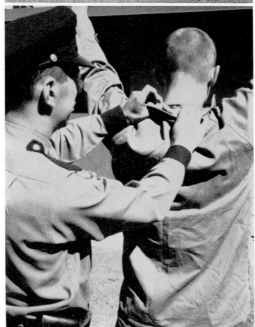

Fig. 10

Fig. 11

Fig. 12

Fig. 13

Fig. 14

Fig. 15

Fig. 16

Fig. 17

Fig. 18

Fig. 19

Fig. 20

Fig. 21

Fig. 22

Fig. 23

Fig. 24

Fig. 25

Fig. 26

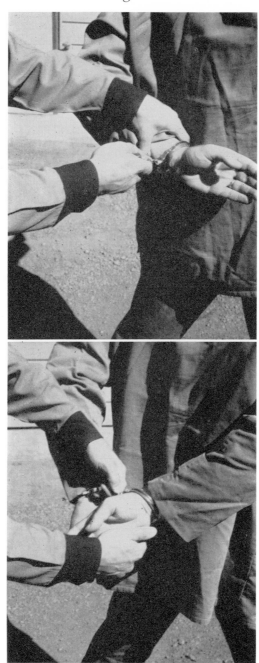

Fig. 27

Fig. 28

Chapter 3

THE SINGLE WALL SEARCH

THE SINGLE WALL search is one of the safest methods of searching a subject. It can be applied when the patrolman is by himself or it can be used when he is accompanied by another officer. Techniques in this book will be demonstrated when a partner is present.

The single wall search is applied on one man. For searching more than one man the group wall search should be applied. This will be covered by Chapter 3. A car may be used in place of a wall if no wall is available when you are searching.

The subject is caught and told to raise his hands high into the air (Fig. 29). He is then approached by one officer to carry our searching maneuvers. The other officer stands to the side and covers the subject (Fig. 30). The covering officer must at all times be alert. He also should stand to the side instead of directly behind the subject. (If the subject is being searched on his left side the covering officer should move to the right side.)

The searching police officer approaches cautiously and gives commands to the subject (Fig. 31). The first command is to have the subject spread his feet apart and point his toes outward (Fig. 32). The second command is to have the subject place his hands down low on the wall with his fingers pointed in an outward direction (Fig. 33). Next the subject should be told to lower his head (Fig. 34).

Now the searching officer must advance with caution and prepare to search the subject. The officer must lock his foot in front of the subject's foot (Figs. 35 and 36). When the foot is locked, if the subject should wish to hit you or perform other physical violence, you can pull his foot out from under him and then prepare for more subduing action (Figs. 37 and 38).

The first of the searching technique is to remove the subject's hat and search its insides (Figs. 39 and 40). Next search the subject's hair and head (Fig. 41). After finishing with the hair search his collar. When doing a wall search, search only one half of the subject at a time. This is the half closest to you. In this instance it would be the subject's left side since the initial search started there (Fig. 42).

In searching don't forget to crush the clothing. Don't pat it. Next search the left side of the subject's back (Fig. 43). After searching the back, search the side and front of the subject (Figs. 44 and 45).

Now have the subject remove his left hand and place it in the small of his back. Search the hand between the fingers and the sleeve and arm (Figs. 46, 47 and 48) The subject should now be instructed to place his hand back on the wall, and a search of the belt should be started (Fig 49).

Now the back and front left pockets should be searched (Figs. 50 and 51). As articles are found they may be either tossed in the hat or upon the ground in one central location.

The crotch should be searched next (Fig. 52). The officer should next either kneel down and check the lower leg area or have the subject raise his leg (Figs. 53 and 54). For checking socks, shoes, etc., the subject should lift his foot (Fig. 55). A good check should be made of the stocking and shoe (Figs. 56 and 57).

The subject is now ready to be searched on the right side. The searcher should back away and have the subject remain as he is (Fig. 58). The searcher should now cross behind the other officer. It is very important not to walk between the subject and the officer guarding him (Fig. 59). As the searcher approaches the other side the cover man should step to the left (Fig. 60).

Again the searcher must lock his foot on the inside of the subject's foot (Fig. 61). Searching now begins with the hair. The searcher should run his fingers through the subject's hair several times (Fig. 62). The right collar should again be searched (Fig. 63).

The subject's back should be checked on the right side (Fig. 64). Also the subject's right side and right front side should be checked (Figs. 65 and 66).

The searcher again should have the subject place his hand (right) in the small of the back (Fig. 67). Here the searcher should check behind and around the fingers and sleeve of the subject (Figs. 68 and 69). The subject must replace his hand on the wall (Fig. 70).

Now the searcher should search the waist and belt area (Fig. 71). The front and back pockets should be gone through (Figs. 72 and 73). Next the crotch and thigh area should be checked (Fig. 74).

After the above is finished, a search of the knee, lower leg, etc. should be made (Fig. 75). At no time should the searcher bend over to search. He should keep his back as straight as possible.

The searcher should have the subject lift his foot so that it may be searched (Fig. 76). The sole and heel should be checked thoroughly (Fig. 77). The socks and shoes should be searched in detail (Figs. 78 and 79). Next the subject should place his foot back on the ground (Fig. 80).

The cuffing process now should be initiated. Have your cuffs ready. Make sure you hold on to one of the cuffs so that he cannot use it as a weapon. Have the subject place his hand on his back and then place the hand cuffs on him (Figs. 81 and 82). Now have him place his other hand on his back and cuff both of his hands (Figs. 83 and 84).

The officer may now assist the subject in standing up against the wall. Since his head is still against the wall and is supporting some of his weight the subject is in a very weak position (Figs. 85 and 86).

Fig. 29

Fig. 30

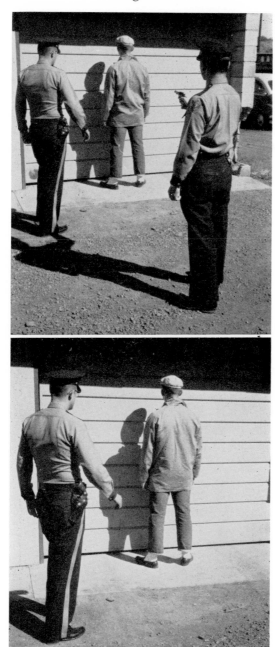

Fig. 31

Fig. 32

Fig. 33

Fig. 34

Fig. 35

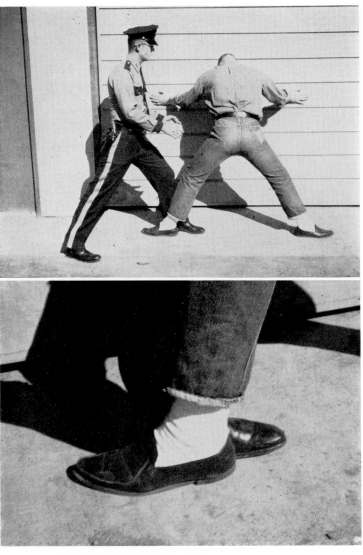

Fig. 36

Fig. 37

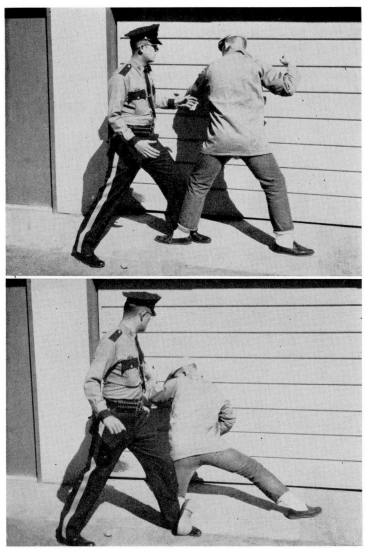

Fig. 38

Fig. 39

Fig. 40

Fig. 41

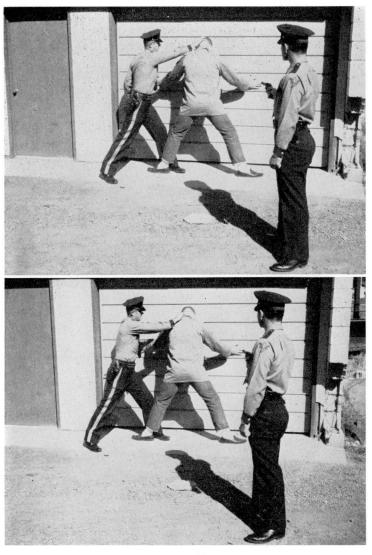

Fig. 42

Fig. 43

Fig. 44

Fig. 45

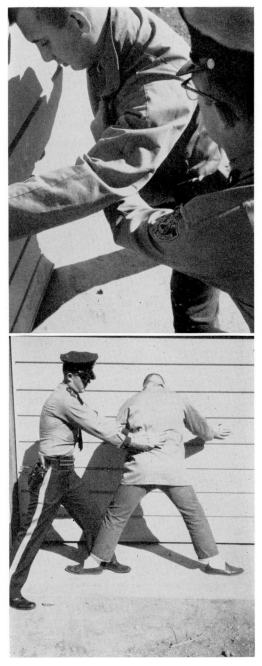

Fig. 46

Fig. 47

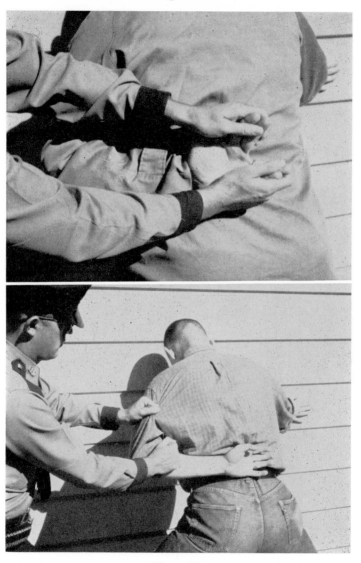

Fig. 48

Fig. 49

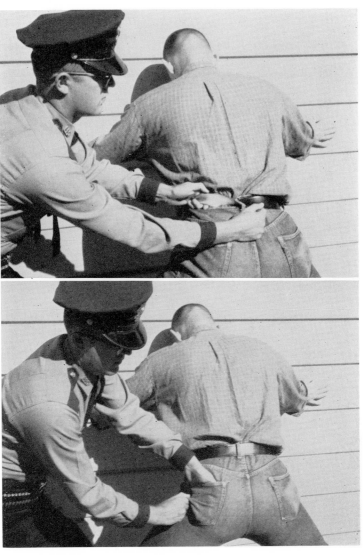

Fig. 50

Fig. 51

Fig. 52

Fig. 53

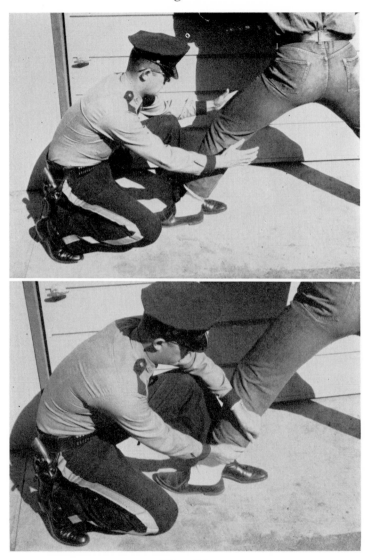

Fig. 54

Fig. 55

Fig. 56

Fig. 57

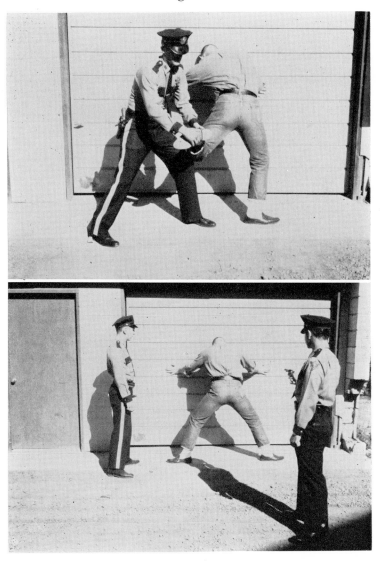

Fig. 58

Fig. 59

Fig. 60

Fig. 61

Fig. 62

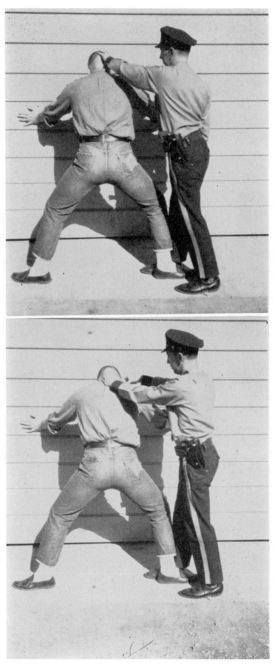

Fig. 63

Fig. 64

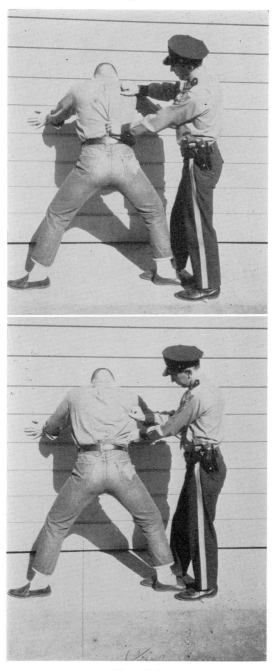

Fig. 65

Fig. 66

Fig. 67

Fig. 68

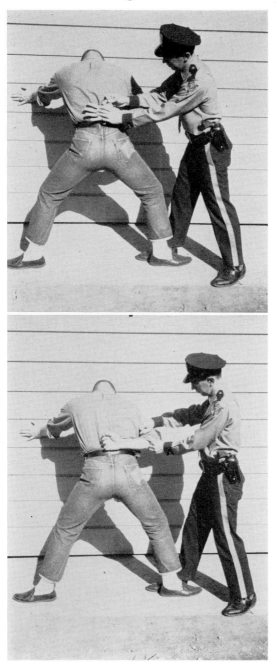

Fig. 69

Fig. 70

Fig. 71

Fig. 72

Fig. 73

Fig. 74

Fig. 75

Fig. 76

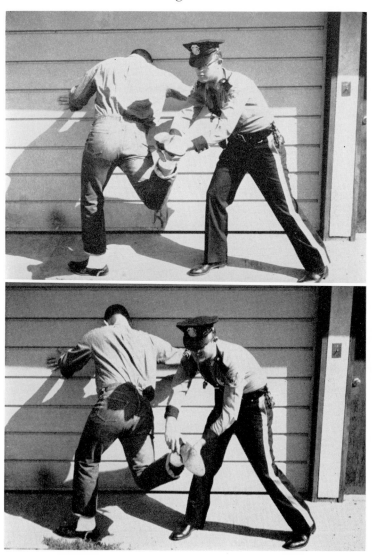

Fig. 77

Fig. 78

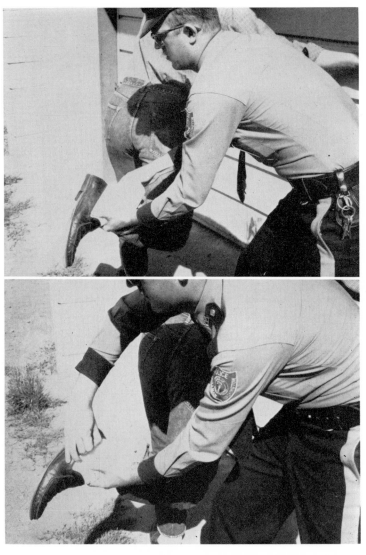

Fig. 79

Fig. 80

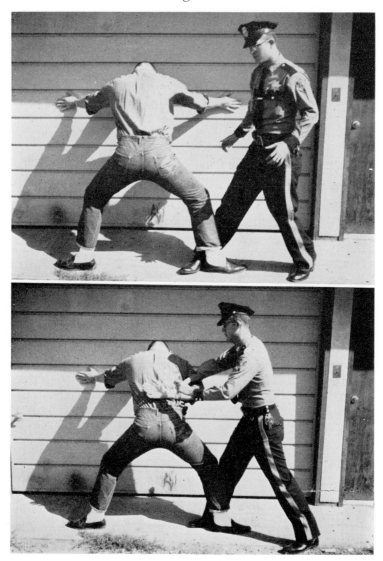

Fig. 81

Fig. 82

Fig. 83

Fig. 84

Fig. 85

Fig. 86

Chapter 4

THE GROUP WALL SEARCH

THE GROUP WALL search is utilized when searching two or more subjects.

Certain general rules prevail when using the group wall search. The following is a brief list of these rules.

Have the subjects out of reach of each other. If they are too close to each other there is a possibility that something could be passed between them.

If you are guarding the subjects don't let one get your attention. This can be very dangerous for the searcher.

Don't let more than one man move at a time. If several men are lined up to be searched let only one man move at a time. If more than one man is moving distractions may occur, and with them the possibility of trouble.

As in the single wall search, if you are the guard don't let the searcher walk between you and the subjects to be searched. The searcher should *always* walk around behind his partner.

Before searching have the subjects spread apart and face the wall (Fig. 87). Next have the subjects spread their feet apart, toes pointing out. Spread their hands out with fingers extended outward and have them place their heads down (Fig. 88). Search first the subject on the left side. Have the guard stand to the right so that he has a good view of both subjects (Fig. 89).

After searching the left side of subject one, cross behind the guard and search the right side of subject two (Figs. 90, 91 and 92). At this time the guard should move over to the left of the subject.

Now that subject one's left side and subject two's right side have been searched it is time for the subjects to switch positions. First have subject one stand up and back away from the wall (Fig. 93). Now have subject two slide over to the position vacated by subject one. (The searcher should be standing back while the subjects are moving (Fig. 94). Now have subject one go to the wall where subject two was and have the searcher search the right side of subject one (Fig. 95). Now subject one has been searched on both sides.

Next the searcher must cross behind the guard and search the left side of subject two, thus completing his search. At this time the guard should move to the right of the subjects (Figs. 96, 97, and 98).

If more than two subjects are to be searched, one subject could be made to lie on the ground during the search of the others (Fig. 99). This, of course, depends upon the nature of the subjects. Those not so dangerous may be made to stand along the wall instead of spread out on the ground. The subject lying down should be made to lie "spread-eagled" on the ground (Figs. 100 and 101). The guard is responsible for the subject on the ground as well as the subjects standing. He should therefore be careful and watchful.

Fig. 87

Fig. 88

Fig. 89

Fig. 90

Fig. 91

Fig. 92

Fig. 93

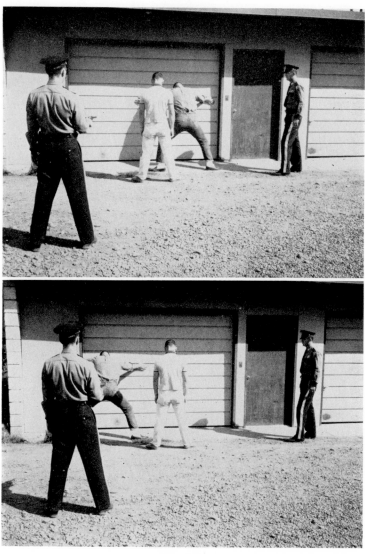

Fig. 94

Fig. 95

Fig. 96

Fig. 97

Fig. 98

Fig. 99

Fig. 100

Fig. 101

Chapter 5

THE STRIP SEARCH

THE STRIP SEARCH better known as the complete search, is the most thorough method of searching.

This search should be conducted in a closed room. This way the searchers know who is present and also they have a better method of keeping track of the subject.

The searchers should not enter the room with weapons. This again is further protection for them.

At least two searchers should be conducting the search. (For women there should be only female attendants during the search; for men just male attendants during the search.)

The strip search may disclose objects the searchers were completely unaware of. It is important to search very carefully in order to find all of the objects which may be concealed.

Have the subject remove all of his clothes and jewelry. These should then be placed in a pile in the room. All of his personal belongings should be completely searched and all clothing thoroughly look at, utilizing the crush method. This will bring forward any materials hidden in the linings, etc. of the clothes.

Next search the subject systematically. Begin with the hair, using a comb. Comb carefully since certain small objects (narcotics) may be hidden in long hair.

The ear opening and area behind the ear should be searched next. Check to make sure nothing is taped behind or in the ears.

Probe the mouth with a tongue depressor. A careful check of the teeth should be made.

Examine the nasal opening with your tongue depressor. Make sure there is nothing jammed up within the nose.

Check very carefully and make sure there is nothing taped or glued to the neck, arms, chest, back of elbows, between the fingers, legs, toes, crotch, etc. Search slowly so that nothing is missed.

Finally, after completely searching the subject, his clothes and jewelry, you may return his clothing and personal effects to him. If you are planning to book and jail the subject, return his clothes minus the belt, shoe strings, neck tie and personal belongings such as watch, etc.

Chapter 6

COME ALONG TECHNIQUES

AFTER SUBDUING AN individual the officer may have to forcibly transport the subject from one location to another. If no handcuffs are available the come alongs contained in this chapter will be extremely helpful. Three come alongs are presented for the use of the reader.

The come alongs should be studied until the officer is sure he can apply them. It is necessary to practice come alongs with a partner. When practicing with another person be very careful in applying your come along. Any rapid movements might endanger the physical well being of your partner.

The Double Finger Come Along

1. You are facing the subject (Fig. 102).
2. Reach with your right hand and grasp two of the subject's right hand fingers (Fig. 103). Now begin bending the fingers back.
3. At the same time you grasp the fingers, with your left hand grab your opponent at the wrist joint (Fig. 104).
4. Apply pressure by bending the fingers back and pulling the opponent's arm from his body. You will now be able to protect yourself from an attack by merely applying pressure before your opponent kicks or attacks (Fig. 105).

The Split Finger Come Along

1. You are again facing the subject (Fig. 106).
2. Reach with your left hand and grab two fingers on your opponent's right hand. Make sure your thumb is in the palm of his hand (Figs. 107 and 108).

[69]

3. With your right hand grasp your opponent's last two fingers. Begin pulling back on the fingers. Make sure your thumbs are on the inside of his palm (Fig. 109).

4. Pull your opponent's arm away from his body, thus locking the elbow joint. The pressure now exerted must be toward the back and in a sideward direction. When properly applied this causes a great deal of pain (Fig. 110).

Reverse Bent Wrist Come Along

1. You face your opponent (Fig. 111).

2. With your right hand grab your opponent's right hand. In grabbing his hand place your hand over the back of it (Fig. 112). Twist his hand up so that his fingers are facing upward (Fig. 113). At the same time you are capturing his hand step to his right side and out slightly (Fig. 114).

3. Pivot on your right foot and bring your left foot next to your opponent's right side (Fig. 115).

4. Now place your left hand between your opponent's arm and his body. Lay your left hand over your right hand and apply pressure directed backward (Figs. 116 and 117).

Fig. 102

Fig. 103

Fig. 104

Fig. 105

Fig. 106

Fig. 107

Fig. 108

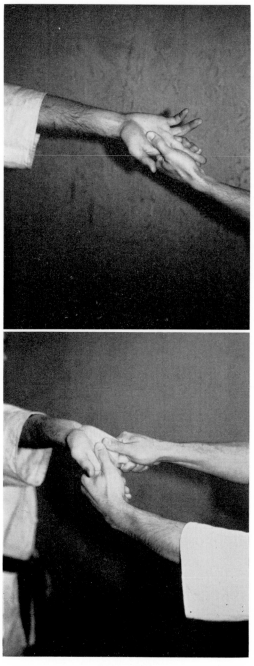

Fig. 109

Fig. 110

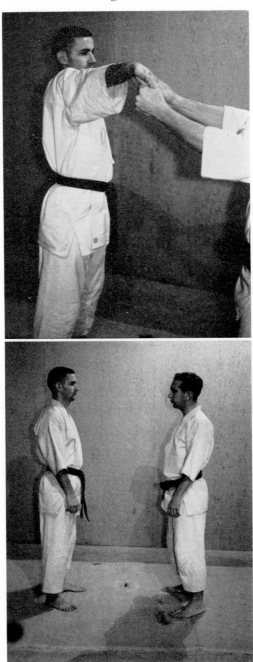

Fig. 111

Fig. 112

Fig. 113

Fig. 114

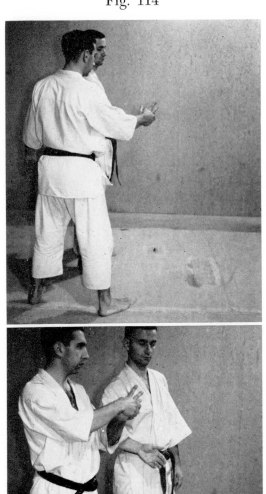

Fig. 115

Fig. 116

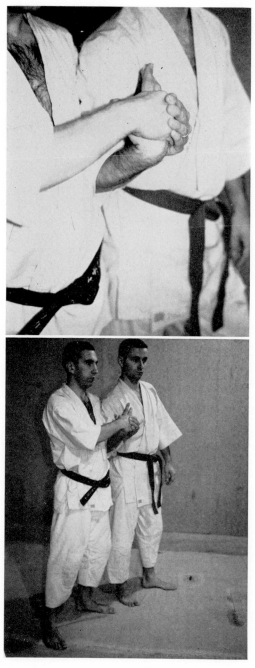

Fig. 117